Table of Contents

Michelle

Do you know
Michelle Obama?

She is famous!

President
Obama

You might know her husband.

He was president.

She was the First Lady.

She helps many people.
She visits shelters.

veteran

INVICTUS GAMES
ORLANDO 2016

INVICTUS GAMES COMING AMERICA

8

She helps veterans.

She supports them.

Michelle is a lawyer.
She is a writer, too.

She writes books!

She cares about kids.

She gets them moving!

Michelle travels.

She is on the go!

She gives speeches.

15

People love Michelle.
She is smart.
She is kind.

Her picture is in a museum.

People look at it.

picture

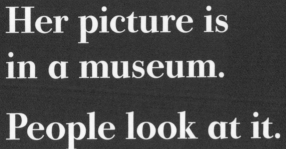

18

Michelle works hard.

19

She gives and gives.
Thank you, Michelle!

21

Key Events

January 20, 2009:
Michelle officially becomes the First Lady of the United States.

January 17, 1964:
Michelle LaVaughn Robinson is born in Chicago, Illinois.

May 29, 2012:
American Grown, Michelle's book about gardening at the White House, is released.

1988:
Michelle graduates from Harvard Law School. She starts working at a law firm in Chicago.

February 9, 2010:
Michelle announces her *Let's Move!* initiative to help keep kids healthy.

July 25, 2016:
Michelle gives a powerful speech at the Democratic National Convention.

Picture Glossary

famous
Very well-known to many people.

shelters
Places where people who are in need can go to for food, shelter, or safety.

First Lady
The wife of the president of the United States.

speeches
Talks given to audiences.

lawyer
A person who has studied law and is trained to advise people in court.

veterans
People who have served in the armed forces.

Index

To Learn More

Learning more is as easy as 1, 2, 3.

1) Go to www.factsurfer.com

2) Enter "MichelleObama" into the search box.

3) Click the "Surf" button to see a list of websites.

With factsurfer.com, finding more information is just a click away.